K - 3

D0856147

United States Air Force

by Julie Murray

www.abdopublishing.com

Published by Abdo Kids, a division of ABDO, PO Box 398166, Minneapolis, Minnesota 55439.

Printed in the United States of America, North Mankato, Minnesota.

052014

092014

 THIS BOOK CONTAINS RECYCLED MATERIALS

Photo Credits: Getty Images, Pixabay, Shutterstock, Thinkstock,
© Keith McIntyre p.1, Chris Parypa Photography p.5 / Shutterstock

Production Contributors: Teddy Borth, Jennie Forsberg, Grace Hansen

Design Contributors: Candice Keimig, Laura Rask, Dorothy Toth

Library of Congress Control Number: 2013953951

Cataloging-in-Publication Data

Murray, Julie.

United States Air Force / Julie Murray.

p. cm. -- (U.S. Armed Forces)

ISBN 978-1-62970-093-9 (lib. bdg.)

Includes bibliographical references and index.

1. United States Air Force--Juvenile literature.   I. Title.

358.400973--dc23

2013953951

Table of Contents

United States Air Force

The Air Force is a branch of the U.S. **Armed Forces**. They use planes to keep America safe.

5

Jobs

All men and women in the

Air Force are called **airmen**.

Some people train to become **officers**. Only officers can fly planes.

8

There are other jobs in the Air Force too. Mechanics keep planes safely flying.

11

Air controllers guide planes.

Doctors and nurses keep

airmen healthy.

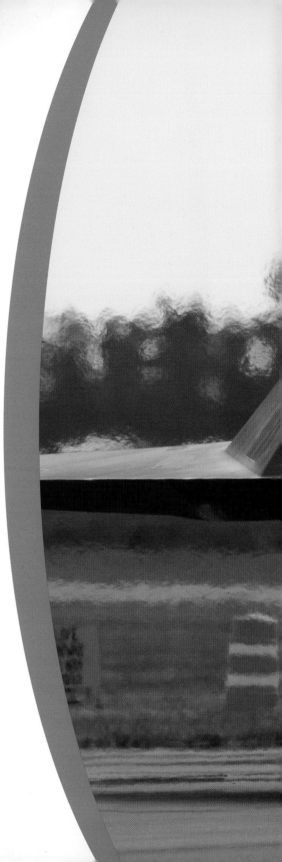

13

Planes

The Air Force uses many
different planes. They
use bomber planes.

They use fighter planes.

They use helicopters too.

17

The Air Force also uses **drone** planes. They are flown by remote controls.

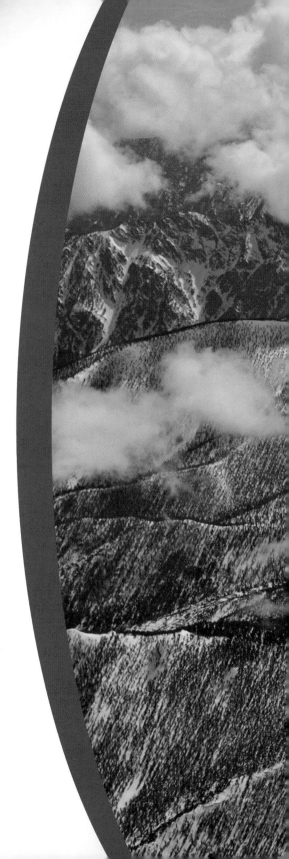

19

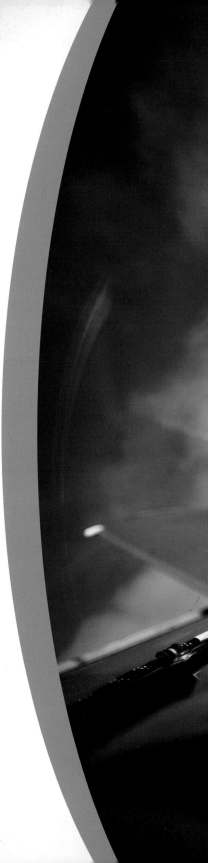

"Aim High ... Fly-Fight-Win"

The Air Force keeps Americans safe every day!

20

More Facts

- Two U.S. Presidents, Ronald Reagan and George W. Bush, joined the U.S. Air Force.

- The Air Force uses fighter jets to support ground troops.

- The U.S. Air Force does not just serve the United States Military. They help those in need with air deliveries. Delivery by air gets supplies to people faster.

Glossary

airman – an enlisted person in the U.S. Air Force.

armed forces – military (land), naval (sea), and air forces (air). They protect and serve their nation.

drone – an aircraft that is remote controlled.

officer – a person who holds a position of authority.

Index

abdokids.com

Use this code to log on to abdokids.com and access crafts, games, videos and more!

Abdo Kids Code:
UUK0939